♥

Give
a little
Love

♥

Give
a little
Love

Written and adapted by Angie Sage
Illustrated by Valeria Petrone

ELEMENT
CHILDREN'S BOOKS

SHAFTESBURY, DORSET•BOSTON, MASSACHUSETTS• MELBOURNE, VICTORIA

First published in 1999 by Element Children's Books
Shaftesbury, Dorset SP7 8BP

Published in the USA in 2000 by Element Books Inc.
160 North Washington Street, Boston MA 02114

Published in Australia in 1999 by Element Books Limited and
distributed by Penguin Books Australia Ltd,
487 Maroondah Highway, Ringwood, Victoria 3134

The Selfish Giant is adapted from the original fairy story by Oscar Wilde;
The Little Mermaid is adapted from the original fairy story
by Hans Christian Andersen

Printed and bound in China

British Library Cataloguing in Publication data available.
Library of Congress Cataloging in Publication data available.

ISBN 1 902618 60 2

Cover and text design by Mandy Sherliker.

CONTENTS

For Laurie and Lois
with love **A.S.**

To Caterina **V.P.**

Love is:

Like a bright butterfly in the Sun,

Like warm toes by the fire,

Like buttered toast,

Like a soft rabbit,

Like cuddles,

Like my Granny.

Maisie
and Dave

There were once two penguins who lived beside the penguin pool at the zoo. They had been together from the time that their mothers used to stand next to each other when they were eggs. They had hatched on the same day, learned to swim together, caught their first fish together and, now that they were grown up, they shared a little cave in the rock beside the penguin pool.

Every morning at the penguin pool a zoo keeper came and brought all the penguins big buckets of fish. He called the two penguins Maisie and Dave. The two penguins called him Fishbucket although he never answered to his name. But then Maisie and Dave never answered to their names either.

Maisie and Dave loved diving for fish. Sometimes Dave swam down to the bottom of the pool and brought up a fish just for Maisie. Sometimes Maisie caught a fish and gave it to Dave. Then they stood on the side of the pool and ate their fish together.

Dave was a short fat penguin and Maisie was a tall thin penguin but they both had bright orange feet and yellow beaks. Dave liked Maisie's yellow beak and Maisie liked Dave's orange feet. There wasn't much to do around the penguin pool but Dave and Maisie were perfectly happy as long as they could stand next to each other and talk about fish, although for the last few weeks Dave and Maisie had been talking about a big black fence that had been put up along one side of the penguin pool.

Sometimes Dave said, "I wonder what that fence is for?"

And sometimes Maisie said, "I wonder what's on the other side?"

In the evening when it got dark Dave and Maisie would go back to their cave by the side of the penguin pool and watch all the people in the zoo go home. Then they would close their eyes and fall asleep together.

But one morning when Dave woke up and said, "Hello Maisie." There was no reply. Maisie had gone.

At first Dave thought that Maisie had gone swimming without him, so he went down to the penguin pool to find her. But Maisie wasn't there. So Dave went back to the cave to see if maybe she had been there all along. But Maisie wasn't there either.

Then Dave ran all the way around the penguin enclosure as fast as his flippers would carry him, he shouted Maisie's name at the top of his voice but there was no reply. Maisie had disappeared.

Dave asked the other penguins if they had seen Maisie but no one had, although some of the other penguins had gone too. Dave was so upset that he did not know what to do. He walked around and around the penguin pool all day calling out Maisie's name but no one answered.

At feeding time Dave could not eat any fish. He pecked Fishbucket's leg to try to make him say where Maisie had gone but Fishbucket didn't say anything, although Dave was sure that Fishbucket knew where Maisie was. So while

all the other penguins were eating their fish, Dave thought
of a plan. When Fishbucket opened the gate to leave,
Dave squeezed out after him.

"Hey!" yelled Fishbucket as he chased Dave.

"Gotcha!" said Fishbucket as he caught up with Dave and
popped him into the empty fish bucket.

"MAISIE!" shouted Dave at the top of his voice, and as
Fishbucket carried Dave back to the penguin pool, Dave
thought that he heard a faint reply, "Dave ..."

That night, alone in the cave, Dave could not sleep.
The more he thought about it the more he was sure that
he had heard Maisie. But where was she? All night long
Dave wandered around the penguin pool; he watched the
moon shine on the water and wondered what the strange
feeling inside him was. It sat just above his tummy and it
made him feel sick. Dave wondered if it was because he
hadn't eaten any fish that day but he knew what it really
was. It was the missing-Maisie feeling inside him.

At last, when it was nearly morning, Dave fell asleep

beside the big black fence.

The next morning was a busy morning at the penguin pool but Dave was so tired he stayed fast asleep. Fast asleep while Fishbucket took away the big black fence, fast asleep until someone said,

"Dave!"

Dave opened his eyes and thought he was dreaming. There was Maisie standing beside him by a beautiful new penguin pool.   "It's me Dave," said Maisie, "I've missed you so much ..." "This is a wonderful dream," said Dave, "I don't want it to end."

"It's not a dream, it's real, this is the other side of the

big black fence," said Maisie, jumping up and down excitedly. "Fishbucket brought me here yesterday morning while I was still asleep. I was so sad, I thought I was never going to see you again."

"I was sad too," said Dave, hopping from one foot to the other, "but I'm so happy now."

"So am I," said Maisie. "Come and see our new pool."

Dave followed Maisie all around the beautiful new penguin pool; they swam in the clear water and slid down the new slide. They climbed the rocks beside the pool and Maisie showed Dave their new cave. It was wonderful. But Dave and Maisie thought that the most wonderful thing of all was being back together again.

Dave and Maisie are old penguins now but they are still there together, standing by the pool, talking about fish and the day that Maisie came back.

Love is missing you
when you're
not there

Frog
Prince

If you had been sitting beside a cool deep pool one summer morning a very long time ago, you might have seen a princess, and you might even have seen a frog. Of course you would have to have been sitting at this particular pool, and you would have to have chosen this particular summer morning.

The princess liked to kick a ball around. Her mother, the queen, had given her a wonderful golden ball that always headed straight for the goal. This was a good thing as the princess never did manage to kick the ball straight, however hard she tried. The only reason she was in the castle soccer team was because it was *her* ball.

On this particular summer morning that we are talking about, the princess was practicing her goal kicks. She was aiming at a large oak tree to the right of the pool. Of course without any goal posts to guide it, the ball had no

idea where it was meant to be going so it just went where the princess kicked it. Straight into the deep, cool pool. Where the frog lived.

The frog was asleep at the time but it soon woke up when a large, golden soccer ball hit it on the head. It looked up crossly and saw the princess peering into the pool. The frog stopped being cross and started thinking how lovely the princess looked.

"Can I have my ball back, please?" asked the princess.

"Yes," said the frog, who thought she had beautiful curly hair.

"Oh thank you, frog," said the princess.

"But," said the frog.

"But what?" asked the princess.

The frog gulped.

He was afraid to ask but he knew he had to. "Um. But. But only if you will take me home with you. Only if you let me live with you, eat supper with you, and only if you let me sleep on your pillow."

Silly frog, thought the princess. But she wanted her ball back so much that she said,

"Yes. All right."

"Promise?" asked the frog.

"Promise," said the princess. "Can I have my ball back now please?"

So the frog threw the ball out of the pool and the princess was so excited to have it back that she ran straight back to the castle and forgot all about the frog.

But the frog did not forget about the princess.

That evening when the princess was having supper with her mother and father, the queen and the king, she heard a flippy floppy sound coming towards the dining room where they were eating. Then she heard a quiet tap-tap at the door. The princess ran to open it. It was the frog.

The frog sat on the cold marble floor outside the door and said, "Remember the promise you made to me; let me in to have my tea."

The princess screamed and slammed the door shut.

The king looked up. "Whers a marrer ear?" he asked with his mouth full of potato.

"What?" said the princess.

The king swallowed the potato and said, "What's the matter, dear?"

"It's that frog," the princess said unhappily.

"What frog?" asked the queen sharply. She didn't like slippery things. Neither did the princess much.

"Oh, this frog gave me my ball back but I promised him that he could come and live with me and have supper and sleep on my pillow ..."

The princess faltered. It all sounded so silly now.

"You promised a *frog*?" asked the queen, her eyebrows shooting up to meet her crown.

The princess looked down at her feet.

She felt very silly.

"Yes," she said.

The king put down his knife and fork. He sighed.

"Well," he said, "If you promised a frog, then you must keep your promise, frog or not. Ask him to come in and have supper."

So the frog had supper with them. He was very polite and the king and queen rather liked him. The princess still felt silly but the frog sat on her plate and gazed at her with his big green eyes in a way that made her feel a bit happier after a while. He also ate all her cabbage for her which meant she could eat two helpings of pudding.

After supper the frog yawned and stretched his little slippery arms above his head, "I'm sleepy now, it's time for bed. Show me the pillow where you lay your head."

The queen looked shocked, "I don't think you should have that frog sleeping on your pillow, dear," she said. "It's not very hygienic."

But the king said, "A promise is a promise, my dear. It must be kept."

So the princess carried the frog up to her room and sat him on her pillow.

"Good night, princess," said the frog.

"Good night, frog," said the princess.

The frog lay down on the pillow and closed his eyes. Soon the princess was fast asleep too; she felt strangely safe and happy with the frog beside her.

The next morning the frog was sitting on the window ledge when the princess woke up.

"Good morning, princess," he said. "It's a beautiful day."

The princess sat up in bed. She was pleased the frog was still there. "It's a lovely day," she agreed.

The frog and the princess spent a happy day together.

She showed him how to play soccer and he showed her how to dive into the river. He told her frog jokes and she told him elephant jokes and they laughed so much that the princess rolled down the river bank and had to be rescued by the frog. The day sped by and before the princess knew it, it was time for supper with the king and queen.

That night the frog again slept on the princess's pillow.

"Good morning, princess. It's a beautiful day," said the frog when the princess woke up. He thought what lovely brown eyes she had.

"Good morning, frog," said the princess. "It's a lovely day." She thought what lovely green eyes he had.

That morning they picked some strawberries in the castle garden and then ate them all. The princess sang the frog her best song and the frog sang it back to the princess. It was his best song too.

In the afternoon they went out together in the princess's boat. The frog told stories while the princess giggled and rowed the boat in circles.

That evening a tired and happy princess had supper with the frog, the king and the queen. Later, as the frog fell asleep on her pillow, the princess closed her eyes and felt very happy. When you are a princess in a big castle it is not always easy to find a good friend and the princess had always felt a little lonely. Until now. Now she had her own best friend. He may have been smaller and greener than she had thought a friend would be, but he was much more fun than she could ever have imagined.

But the next morning when the princess woke up, the frog had gone. Lying on her pillow was a handsome prince with lovely green eyes.

"Good morning, princess," said the handsome prince, "It's a beautiful day."

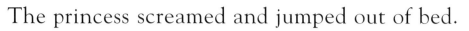

The princess screamed and jumped out of bed.

The king and queen heard her scream and ran to the room. They threw open the door and the queen screamed too. Then the princess screamed again to keep her company.

"WHAT IS GOING ON?" yelled the king above all the screaming.

"My frog," yelled the princess, "My frog's gone. He's taken my frog!" She pointed at the handsome prince with green eyes.

The prince sat up in bed. He looked flustered.

"But that was me. I was your frog and now you have set me free. Now I am myself again, a handsome prince."

"I wouldn't say handsome exactly," scowled the princess. "Although I suppose you have nice green eyes. My frog had nice green eyes. Well, nicer really."

The prince got out of bed. "These eyes you see are the same," he said. "I tell you, dear princess, I was that frog."

"Nonsense," snapped the queen. "I bet you say that whenever you get caught."

"Let me tell you what happened," said the handsome prince, "Then you will understand."

The king, the queen and the princess sat down and folded their arms.

"Some time ago," said the handsome prince, "I had the misfortune to offend a thirteenth fairy. You know the kind, the ones that hang around hoping you will do something to annoy them. Unfortunately I accidentally trod upon this fairy's toe. At once she put a spell on me. She turned me into a frog and left me at the bottom of the pool where you found me. I was to live there as a frog forever unless a princess let me stay with her, gave me food for three days, and let me sleep upon her pillow for three nights. Only then could I resume my former self."

"How awful," whispered the queen to the king.

"For months, years maybe, I sat in the bottom of the pool. I was in despair. How could I ever find a princess to take an ugly frog home with her?"

"You weren't ugly. You were a very good-looking frog. Of course I took you home with me," said the princess, conveniently forgetting how she had left the frog to find his own way to the castle. "And you were my best friend," she added, a little sadly.

The prince bowed and said, "perhaps I may still be your best friend?"

The princess looked into the prince's green eyes. He was, she decided, just about as nice as her frog had been.

"You might," she said, "when I

know you better. Fancy a game of soccer?"

"You bet," said the handsome prince.

"You can be in goal," said the princess.

"Well," said the queen, when the prince and princess had gone, "I don't think I'll ever look at frogs in quite the same way again."

"No," agreed the king, "or anything else for that matter. It makes you wonder about her goldfish, doesn't it?"

"Still," said the queen, "as long as they're happy."

And the funny thing is, they were. Very happy.

Love doesn't mind if
you're a frog or
a prince

Lovelist

I love:
-Chocolate
-Puddles
-Elephants
-The smell of new books
-Spaceships
-Wet sand when the tide goes out
-My penguin socks
-To hold my brand new baby sister
and watch her fall asleep.

Little Seed

When Sophie found a seed she asked her Granny how to make it grow.

"The same way as you make people grow," said Granny. "Lots of love, sunshine, good food, and a warm bed to lie in."

So Sophie took the seed and cuddled it in her hand. She took it out for a walk in the sun, she read it a story, and she told it her funniest jokes. At suppertime she gave it some of her chips and at night she wrapped it up in tissue and took it to bed with her. But it didn't grow.

"Well," said Granny, when Sophie asked her why the seed wouldn't grow, "You're giving it lots of love, but it needs its own kind of food and bed."

Granny showed Sophie how to plant the seed.
They found a little flowerpot and filled it with earth.
Then they took it indoors and let the earth get warm.

"No one likes getting into a cold bed," said Granny.

LITTLE SEED

27

When the earth was warm Sophie poked a little hole in it with her finger and dropped the seed in. Then she covered up the seed with some of the earth.

"Now it needs something to drink," said Granny. So Sophie poured a little bit of water over the earth for the seed to drink.

"What do we give it to eat?" she asked.

"Nothing yet," said Granny. "It is only a baby. Soon the water will make it swell up and then it will take its food from the earth."

Sophie put the little flowerpot on the windowsill in her bedroom so that it would get some warm sunshine. Then she waited.

Every day Sophie looked in the flowerpot but there was nothing to see. After a while Sophie didn't look so often. When Granny came over a few weeks later, Sophie showed her the flowerpot.

"It's not doing anything," she said. "Is it ill?"

Granny touched the earth which had shrunk away from the sides of the pot and was now hard like a stone.

"It's thirsty," said Granny. "It needs water. And it needs caring for every day, not just sometimes."

Sophie and Granny stood the dry little pot in a bowl of water and watched the earth swell up again and become soft. Then they put it back on the windowsill. Sophie put a little jug of water beside the pot so that she would remember to water it. "Sorry I forgot about you," she told the seed under the earth.

Sophie kept the earth damp with a few drops of water every day and one morning she saw a little green blob pushing its way up through the earth.

"Hello, little plant," she said.

The next day the green blob was taller. The day after that it was taller still. Soon it had two little leaves, then four, then six big leaves. Then it fell over.

"It's too big for its pot," said Granny, "Why don't we put it in the garden?" So Sophie and Granny put the straggly plant into a sunny flower bed underneath Sophie's bedroom window.

Now every morning Sophie looked down from her bedroom window and said, "Hello, little plant." And every morning it seemed to her that the plant was a bit taller.

Now that the plant was outside it had plenty of sunshine and water from the rain. It grew so well that it was soon taller than Sophie, then Granny. Its leaves grew bigger and a large bud appeared at the top of it. Sophie

At last her fifteenth birthday arrived. "Now," said her grandmother, "you are ready to see the world above the ocean."

The little mermaid could hardly believe that this was the moment she had waited for for so long. She swam up to the surface of the sea, her long hair broke through the waves, and the little mermaid saw the world above the sea for the first time. It was beautiful.

The sun was low; the sea was calm and shone with dancing reflections from a beautiful three-masted ship.

The little mermaid bobbed in the waves and gazed at the ship. As the sun set, music was played and there was dancing, singing, and laughter. The little mermaid, who had a lovely voice, sang too. A beautiful young prince, whose birthday party it was, leaned out to listen to the singing. The little mermaid looked up at him and, from that moment, she loved him. But all the young prince saw

was some pure white sea foam in the moolight.

Soon the wind began to blow and the waves grew bigger. It was not long before a wild storm was raging and the prince's ship began to break up in the water. The little mermaid should have dived to safety but she could not bear to leave the prince in danger; she knew that humans, unlike mermaids, cannot breathe under the sea.

When she saw her prince struggling to swim, the little mermaid came to him. She held his head above the water and whispered encouraging words to him, but his eyes were closed and he did not reply. All night the little mermaid swam with him until, as the sun rose, she at last found land. She laid the prince gently on a sandy beach and sadly kissed him goodbye, then she swam a little way out and watched to see if anyone would find him.

A little bit later a beautiful young girl walked along the

beach and found the prince. As he opened his eyes the first person he saw was the girl gazing at him.

"You have saved me," he murmured to her. The young girl did not know what to say; she knew she had not saved him but she thought he was very handsome.

From behind the rocks beyond the beach the little mermaid gazed at her prince. She watched him walk up the beach holding the young girl's hand.

Sadly, the little mermaid swam home.

The little mermaid could not stop thinking about the prince. At last she told her grandmother that the only thing she wanted was to be with him.

"But you can't," said her grandmother, "because you have a fish tail instead of two legs. You can't walk on the land."

The little mermaid sighed. She knew what her grandmother said was true.

But as time went on the little mermaid missed the prince more and more. At last she decided to visit the sea witch. The sea witch was powerful and lived in the dark part of the Merman Kingdom.

"What," she asked the little mermaid, "can an old witch do for a beautiful princess who has all she can desire?"

"I do not have all I desire," replied the little mermaid. "I want two legs so that I may walk on the land and see my prince again. I want him to love me and marry me."

The witch laughed. "We always want what we do not have," she said.

"But I want this more than anything in the world," said the little mermaid.

"Well," said the witch, "there is always a price to pay."

And the little mermaid paid it. The sea witch took her tongue in exchange for two human legs. She told the little mermaid that if the prince did not marry her she would die and become foam on the water. It was a high price.

The little mermaid kissed her sisters good-bye, then she swam all the way to the prince's land and pulled herself onto the beach exhausted. It was there that the prince found her. He lifted her to her feet and when she stood up for the first time she wanted to scream. Each step she took was as though she was walking on knives. But the little mermaid was so happy to see the prince that she glided along as though she felt nothing.

The prince asked the little mermaid to live at the palace. He thought she was beautiful and he loved the way she danced so gracefully; he never dreamed how much it hurt her. She longed to tell him how she had saved him from the sinking ship and how much she loved him but of

course she could not speak. The prince often talked to the little mermaid about all the things he cared about, and one day he said, "You must be happy for me, my little silent one. Soon I am to marry the one I love."

The little mermaid felt as though a knife had stabbed her heart; she knew that the prince did not mean her.

The day came when the prince was to marry. The wedding was to be on board a beautiful ship and the little mermaid was invited. When the prince walked on board with his bride the little mermaid gasped, for the prince was marrying the girl who had found him lying on the beach where the little mermaid had gently laid him.

The prince introduced his bride to everyone, saying, "Here is the only one I could ever love. The one who saved me from the waves."

The little mermaid wanted to shout, "But it was I who saved you from the waves, you must love *me*." But she could not because the sea witch had her tongue.

That night the little mermaid danced the last few hours of her life away at the prince's wedding party. When midnight came her sisters rose up from the water singing the saddest song anyone had ever heard, as the little mermaid slipped over the side of the ship and became nothing but pure white sea foam floating on the waves.

Love
hurts

Dear Ted,

I hope you are feeling better. I miss you lots and so does Lois even though it was all her fault in the first place. I hope you will be home soon.

Lois says "sorry" and she wants me to tell you that she didn't mean to leave you in the washbasin but she thought you could swim. Dad says "sorry" too, he says the washing machine was very old and he hopes you weren't frightened by all the smoke. Sheba hasn't said anything at all but she is only a dopey dog so I expect she has forgotten everything by now. The carpet is still soggy but Dad hopes it will dry out soon. The washing machine repairman is coming tomorrow.

I miss you, Ted, but I know you are safe with Granny. Lois and Dad send their love and so do I.

Love from Laurie xxx

P.S. Lots of bear hugs too. You are my BEST BEAR and I love you lots. Please come home soon.

Dear Laurie,

Granny is writing this for me as I don't have my arms back on yet. I am feeling much better thank you. Granny says that Lois was probably trying to teach me to swim in the basin just like she is learning to swim at the baby pool. Granny says that even she forgets to turn the taps off sometimes and has Dad tried using a hair dryer to dry out the carpet?

Granny says that she is sorry the washing machine blew up while Dad was trying to spin me dry and she hopes the repairman will be able to fix it.

I must say that I was scared when Sheba started chewing my arms off but I suppose no one noticed because of all the smoke from the washing machine.

Granny sends her love and says that she has nearly finished knitting my new arms. She is going to make a squeaky ball for Sheba so that she will have something to gnaw instead of me because all puppies need to chew on something when they are teething. I don't mind what Sheba chews on as long as it isn't my new arms.

I miss you too, Laurie. I will be back very soon.

Lots and lots of love,
Ted xxx

(Lots of bear hugs when I get my arms back)

Love mends you when you fall apart

side into a small rocky cove.

"I can see it!" he yelled. "I can see the Egg Pool!"

A few minutes later Jack and Dad were sitting beside a large egg-shaped rock pool. They dangled their feet in the clear greeny-blue water and watched some small fish dart for cover under a rock.

"Shall we go for a swim?" asked Dad.

"I haven't got my arm bands," said Jack. "It looks deep ..." He gazed into the pool. The bottom was covered in sand and looked much deeper than the shallow end in the swimming pool where he'd been having swimming lessons.

"I'll go in first and see," said Dad.

It was deep in the Egg Pool. Dad swam around and dived down under the water while Jack watched. Jack loved the idea of swimming with the fish and touching the sticky little sea anenomes under the water like Dad was. But he couldn't swim. Dad knew that. Jack felt cross with Dad for swimming around without him. It wasn't fair.

"Come on Jack ..." Dad swam to the rock where Jack was sitting. "I'll hold you. In fact I promise you'll be able to swim in here. It's easier to swim in salty water. That's

how I learned. Much easier than a swimming pool."

"Promise?" asked Jack doubtfully.

"Promise." said Dad. "Now look in that green bag in my rucksack."

"Wow, Dad!" Jack took a smart new blue mask and snorkel from out of the bag.

"For you," said Dad. "Just put the mask on for now until you get the hang of things. Spit in it first then wash it out with water."

"Yuk Dad."

"Go on. It'll stop it misting up while you're swimming." Dad held his arms out and Jack slithered into the Egg Pool.

"It's freezing!"

"Soon warm up. Splash about a bit." Jack splashed about and felt warmer. The face mask was great, it stopped the water going in his eyes and stinging like it did in the swimming pool.

"Look at that fish!" said Dad as a bright silver streak darted past them. Jack decided to see if his mask worked. He ducked his head under the water and suddenly the

whole world was different. He could see! He could see everything clearer and brighter than above the water. There was seaweed wafting slowly, little pearly shells glistening and bright red sea anenomes waving at him. Without thinking, Jack let go of Dad and started to paddle over to a sea anenome. He put his finger on the little waving fronds; for a moment they stuck to him and then let go and disappeared into a soft red ball.

"Hey Dad, I touched a sea anenome!"

"Hey Jack," laughed Dad, "You're swimming!"

"I'm swimming! I'm swimming!" Jack paddled slowly around the Egg Pool, then he took a deep breath and let himself sink down under the water. It was beautiful. He waved his arms like a sea anenome and watched the silver air bubbles from his mouth drift up to the surface.

"I can swim," he thought as he floated up to the surface, "I can swim in the sea just like Dad."

I am Me

I like being me because:
I can run fast,
I can wiggle my nose
and I am bigger than my little brother.

I like being me because:
I like the feelings inside me
I like the me inside my head.

I like being me because:
my best friend likes me
because I am me.

Kevin's Leg

Kevin was nosy, that was the trouble. The other trouble was that Rita was very patient. And there was another trouble too, which I suppose was the biggest trouble of all. The biggest trouble of all was – I left the lid off the gerbil cage.

So I know it was my fault that Rita bit off Kevin's leg.

Kevin was the loveliest gerbil ever. When I chose him in the pet shop he was with his brother, Fred. The man in the pet shop said it would be nice to keep them together, so Dad let me buy both. It was a late birthday present from my Granny.

I loved Kevin right from the beginning because he was so nosy. He sniffed my fingers and ran onto my hand, then he stood up and smiled at me. He did, really. After that I just knew that Kevin was special. He loved exploring the cardboard tubes I put into his cage, diving into one end and then sticking his little head out of the other end in no time at all. He was small and had shiny black fur and tiny little ears. Fred was great too, but he was shy and sat inside his box a lot of the time.

I'd had enough money from Granny to buy a really great place for them to live. It was a big plastic box with a lid. But one day when I gave Kevin and Fred their food I forgot to put the lid back on. This is where Rita comes in.

Rita is a fat old cat; she used to spend most of the time sitting on a cushion by the fire, but when I got Kevin and Fred she started sitting on the top of the cupboard next to the table that their box was on. I thought she was just bored and wanted to watch them playing. But now I know that she was waiting for a chance to catch them. Every day Rita sat and looked at Kevin and Fred. She sat for hours and hours. As I said, she was very patient.

The day it all happened I was looking for my reading book. When I opened the door to the room where Kevin and Fred were, Rita rushed out past me and scuttled away. I thought that was odd because Rita never rushes anywhere, she just sits. I said hello to Kevin and Fred, just like I always do, and I noticed the lid was on the floor, so I put it back on. Fred was peeping out of his box but Kevin wasn't doing much, so I said hello again. It was then that I saw it.

Kevin's leg.

At first I thought someone had dropped a weird furry matchstick into the cage, but then I looked at Kevin. He didn't look well. He was sitting in the corner of the cage, shivering. I looked at the furry matchstick again and suddenly I knew what had happened.

"DAD!" I screamed, "Rita's pulled off Kevin's leg!" It sounded so awful when I said it that I felt sick. Kevin looked pretty sick too.

"WHAT?" said Dad, rushing into the room. I pointed at the gerbil cage. Dad took in the scene. In one corner sat Kevin. In the other corner sat Kevin's leg.

"Oh dear," said Dad.

"We've got to take Kevin to the vet. We've got to save him," I said. "It's all my fault, I left the lid off the cage."

Dad didn't look too happy about going to the vet. He'd only just paid the last bill for Rita's fur falling out.

"Please, Dad, PLEASE," I said.

Dad put his arm round me, "OK," he said, "We'll take Kevin to the vet."

I carefully picked Kevin up. He felt very damp and trembly; he lay in the palm of my hand and just looked at me.

"It's OK, Kevin," I whispered to him, even though I wasn't at all sure that it was OK. I laid him on some bedding in an ice cream box and I carried him to the car. It was then I remembered something. I rushed back and got a bag of frozen peas from the freezer. It was already half empty but it was all there was.

Now there was something I had to do. I took a deep breath, went to the gerbil cage and picked up Kevin's leg. It was tiny and didn't feel like it belonged to Kevin anymore, but I held it carefully and put it on the bag of peas.

I held onto Kevin and the bag of peas all the way to the vet. "It's OK, Kevin," I kept whispering but Kevin didn't seem to hear, he just stared at me as though he had forgotten who I was. "Come ON, Dad," I said as he stopped at the main road. We should have had a blue light and a siren; after all, if that had happened to a human there would have been a real fuss. But Dad wouldn't go through any red traffic lights and by the time we got to the vet's Kevin was lying very still and breathing very fast.

They let us go straight in to see the vet. I put the ice cream box in the middle of a big black table and the vet looked at Kevin very carefully. I told her what had happened and laid the bag of peas down beside Kevin. Some of the peas fell out and rolled onto the floor.

The vet looked serious. "Well," she said, "We can either mend him or ..."

"Or what?" I asked.

"Put him to sleep," she said. "He's only a little animal and he's had a big shock."

"Mend him," I told her. "Please."

The vet looked at Dad.

"OK," said Dad. "See what you can do."

"Right," said the vet. "I'll do the best I can. I'm afraid I can't sew his leg back on, it's too small. But he'll be fine with three legs, don't worry. Do you want to stay with him while he goes to sleep?"

So I sat with Kevin while the vet put him into a little plastic box that was attached to some gas. The vet turned on the gas and I saw Kevin go floppy. Then I said goodbye to Kevin. I felt so sad, I thought I might not see him again. Dad put his arm round me and we followed the trail of frozen peas back to the car.

We went home and waited. Every time the phone rang I thought it was going to be about Kevin. But it wasn't. After about an hour I was beginning to think that maybe Kevin was OK ... or maybe not. I just didn't know.

The phone rang again and I jumped.

"You get it this time," said Dad. So I picked it up.

"Hello, this is the vet ..."

"Hello ... is Kevin ...?"

"Kevin is sleepy, but he's fine."

"YAY!" I yelled.

The voice on the end of the phone sounded smiley.

"Everything went well; the vet has sewn up where he lost his leg. You can come and collect him in about an hour or so."

So I went to see Fred. "Kevin's fine!" I told him, "He's coming back soon and he'll need you to look after him." Fred looked at me with his head on one side and then went back in his box.

The funny thing is, Fred did look after Kevin.

That evening when Kevin came home I put him gently onto some clean bedding in the cage and watched as Fred went over to see him. Fred looked at Kevin and Kevin looked at Fred. Then Fred gave Kevin a little lick. I had never seen Fred do that before. Kevin just lay there and Fred started to give Kevin a good wash. He licked Kevin's fur so that it began to shine again. I had never realized before how much Fred loved Kevin.

For the next few days Fred looked after Kevin. He washed him and once I saw him bringing Kevin some food. Kevin spent a lot of time asleep but Fred just sat beside him or curled up next to Kevin and went to sleep too.

Now Kevin is better; Fred still licks Kevin but now Kevin

licks Fred as well. I often see them sitting together now and playing together too. I think they never knew how much they cared about each other until Kevin lost his leg.

Dad paid the vet bill last month but he said he didn't mind at all, he said that Kevin was worth it. Dad doesn't let on but I know he loves Kevin too.

But not as much as I do.

Love
makes you
feel
better

The Selfish Giant

There was once a beautiful garden outside a castle. Every day after school all the children of the town used to play in the garden. There were twelve pear trees in the garden which the children loved to climb. In the spring the trees had wonderful scented blossom which the children loved to smell and in the late Summer they would climb up and eat the delicious pears. There were soft, grassy banks which the children used to roll down and beautiful flowers. The birds sang and the children laughed and played. They loved the garden.

The garden belonged to a Giant. The Giant had been away on holiday for seven years which is the usual amount of time that giants spend on holiday. One day he came back. The ground shook beneath the children's feet, the sky became dark as the Giant's shadow fell across them, and then they heard a noise like thunder.

"GET OUT OF MY GARDEN!" yelled the Giant.

The children ran home screaming.

The Giant put up a big sign in the garden that said,

KEEP OUT

in big red letters. Then he began to build a wall. He built the tallest wall that anyone in the town had ever seen. It went all the way around the garden. There was no gate in the wall because the Giant did not need one. He never went out and no one ever came in.

Now the children had nowhere to play after school. They walked home sadly in the shadow of the Giant's wall and talked about how much fun they had had in the garden.

Winter came, and then spring. In the town the birds sang and the trees blossomed. The sun was warm and the grass began to grow. But not inside the Giant's garden. Inside the Giant's garden, spring never came.

Snow covered the ground and icicles hung from the

trees. The Giant shivered and huddled by his fire. The cold north wind blew through the dark, bare garden; it shook the windows of the Giant's house and kept him awake. Hailstones rattled down the Giant's chimney and put his fire out. The Giant went to bed, wrapped himself up in blankets and stared out of the window miserably.

"Why is spring so late this year?" he wondered.

But spring was not just late, it never came. Neither did summer. For many long years winter stayed in the Giant's garden and the Giant grew sad and weak from staying huddled in bed.

Until one wonderful morning.

When the Giant woke up he heard some beautiful music playing. He thought he might have heard it before, a long time ago, but he could not remember what it was. Then he noticed something else. The hail had stopped jumping in the fireplace, the wind had stopped rattling his windows, and he had stopped shivering under his blankets. He almost felt warm.

The Giant struggled out of bed and looked out of the window. He could not believe his eyes. After all the long years of winter, spring had at last come to his garden. The music he heard was a bird singing. It was singing because children had scrambled back into the garden through a hole in the wall, which was now old and crumbling.

The Giant felt so happy and excited. He rushed out

into his garden. The trees were blossoming and in each tree he saw a child. He ran through the garden looking at the flowers and the green grass and feeling the warmth of the sun after all the long years of winter. Then, in the corner of the garden he found a little patch of winter still there. Standing under the twelfth pear tree was a little boy, crying because he could not reach up to the branches to climb into the tree.

The tree was still covered in snow and frost and a cold wind swirled about the boy. The Giant knelt down and gently picked up the little boy and placed him in the tree.

At once the tree blossomed, the snow melted, and the wind dropped. Spring had reached every corner of the garden.

That day the Giant knocked the wall down so that the

children could once again
play in the garden.

"How selfish I was,"
he said to himself as
he looked at his
beautiful garden in
the sunshine, "to try to
keep all this for myself.
No wonder spring
never came."

Now the Giant looked
forward to hearing the
children come every
day after school. He watched
them play but he never again saw the
little boy he had lifted into the tree.
He missed him, and sometimes asked the
children where he was, but they did not
know who the little boy was at all.

For many long and happy years children played
in the Giant's garden. The Giant grew old and now
spent more time sitting in his chair watching the
children than playing with them as he used to. But
the children loved him; they brought him blossom
in the spring and bunches of flowers in the summer,
and they picked pears for him when they were ripe.

The Giant did not mind winter any more because he knew that spring would always come. So one winter's morning he was happily looking out of the window when he saw a wonderful sight.

He saw the little boy that he had lifted into the tree all those years ago, and whom he had never forgotten. The Giant felt happier than he had ever felt before. He ran out into the garden and found the little boy standing under the twelfth pear tree.

The tree was covered in beautiful flowers and the boy was surrounded by a wonderful light that seemed to come from inside him. Without understanding why, the Giant threw himself down in front of the boy. The boy smiled and said,

"Once you let me play in your garden. Now it is your turn to play in mine. My Garden is called Paradise."

And when all the children came to play that afternoon, they found the Giant lying dead under the twelfth pear tree, which was covered in beautiful flowers.

Love is
learning
to give

There are lots of kinds of love:
Happy love for someone who makes you smile.
Sad love when someone is going away.
Funny love when your dog rolls in the mud.
Cross love when your sister's annoying.
Cuddly love for your teddy at night.
And lots and lots of special love in the
letter from your Dad.

And who
do you love?